Measuring Weather

Copyright © by Harcourt, Inc.

All rights reserved. No part of this publication may be reproduced or transmitted in any form or by any means, electronic or mechanical, including photocopy, recording, or any information storage and retrieval system, without permission in writing from the publisher.

Requests for permission to make copies of any part of the work should be addressed to School Permissions and Copyrights, Harcourt, Inc., 6277 Sea Harbor Drive, Orlando, Florida 32887-6777. Fax: 407-345-2418.

HARCOURT and the Harcourt Logo are trademarks of Harcourt, Inc., registered in the United States of America and/or other jurisdictions.

Printed in Mexico

ISBN-13: 978-0-15-363641-7
ISBN-10: 0-15-363641-6

2 3 4 5 6 7 8 9 10   050   16 15 14 13 12 11 10 09 08

Harcourt
SCHOOL PUBLISHERS

Visit *The Learning Site!*
www.harcourtschool.com

windy

sunny

It may be sunny or windy.

rainy

snowy

It may be rainy or snowy.

You can dress for the weather.

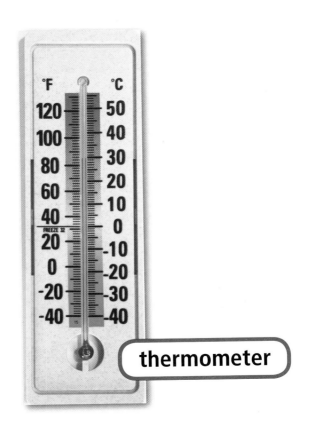

thermometer

This tool shows how warm the air is.

rain gauge

This tool shows how much rain falls.

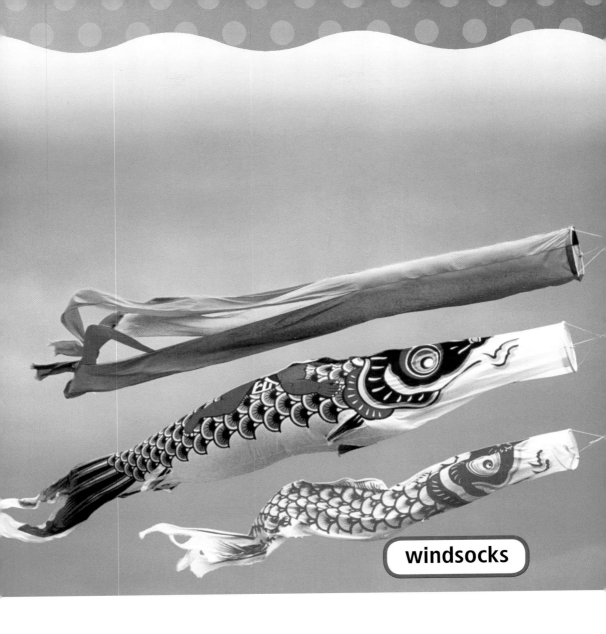

windsocks

You can tell which way wind blows.

We can keep track of weather.